What makes you YOU?

Gill Arbuthnott

ILLUSTRATED BY Marc Mones

Crabtree Pub

www.crab

Crabtree Publishing Company
www.crabtreebooks.com
1-800-387-7650

Published in Canada
Crabtree Publishing
616 Welland Avenue
St. Catharines, ON
L2M 5V6

Published in the United States
Crabtree Publishing
PMB 59051
350 Fifth Ave, 59th Floor
New York, NY 10118

Published by Crabtree Publishing Company in 2016

*For Tom, Ellen, and Robert,
who make me me!*

Author: Gill Arbuthnott

Project coordinator: Kathy Middleton

Editor: Wendy Scavuzzo

Proofreader: Janine Deschenes

Prepress technician: Tammy McGarr

Print and production coordinator:
   Margaret Amy Salter

Science Consultant: Shirley Duke

Text copyright © 2013 Gill Arbuthnott
Illustration copyright © 2013 Marc Mones

Additional picture acknowledgements:
Additional images all Shutterstock, aside from the following: p6 top
right and p58 left © Wikimedia, p6 bottom left and p58 top right ©
Wikimedia, p11 bottom right and p58 left © Wikimedia, p16 top left
and p58 right © BE031947/Corbis, p16 top middle and p59 left © King's
College London, p16 top right and p58 right © BE031947/Corbis, p17 top
right and p58 bottom © Jenifer Glynn, p19 top left © Science Source,
p19 top left © Science Source, p29 bottom right © Wikimedia.

The rights of Gill Arbuthnott and Marc Mones to be identified as the
author and illustrator of this work respectively have been asserted
by them.

First published in 2013 by A & C Black, an imprint of Bloomsbury
Publishing Plc
Copyright © 2013 A & C Black

All Internet addresses given in this book were correct at the time of
going to press. The author and publishers regret any incovenience
caused if addresses have changed or if websites have ceased to exist,
but can accept no responsibility for any such changes.

Printed in Canada/022016/MA20151130

Library and Archives Canada Cataloguing in Publication

Arbuthnott, Gill, author
      What makes you you? / Gill Arbuthnott ; Marc Mones, illustrator.

(Drawn to science, illustrated guides to key science concepts)
Includes index.
ISBN 978-0-7787-2239-7 (bound).--
ISBN 978-0-7787-2247-2 (paperback)

      1. Genetics--Juvenile literature. 2. Genes--Juvenile literature.
3. DNA--Juvenile literature. I. Mones, Marc, illustrator II. Title.

QH437.5.A73 2016   j576.5   C2015-907105-4

Library of Congress Cataloging-in-Publication Data

Names: Arbuthnott, Gill, author. | Mones, Marc, illustrator.
Title: What makes you you? / Gill Arbuthnott ; illustrated by Marc
    Mones.
Description: Crabtree Publishing Company, 2016. | Series: Drawn to
    science: illustrated guides to key science concepts | Includes index.
Identifiers: LCCN 2015042097| ISBN 9780778722397 (reinforced library
    binding : alk. paper) | ISBN 9780778722472 (pbk. : alk. paper)
Subjects: LCSH: DNA--Juvenile literature. | Genetics--Juvenile
    literature. | Heredity--Juvenile literature.
Classification: LCC QP624 .A73 2016 | DDC 572.8/6--dc23
LC record available at http://lccn.loc.gov/2015042097

Contents

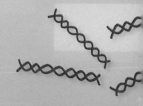

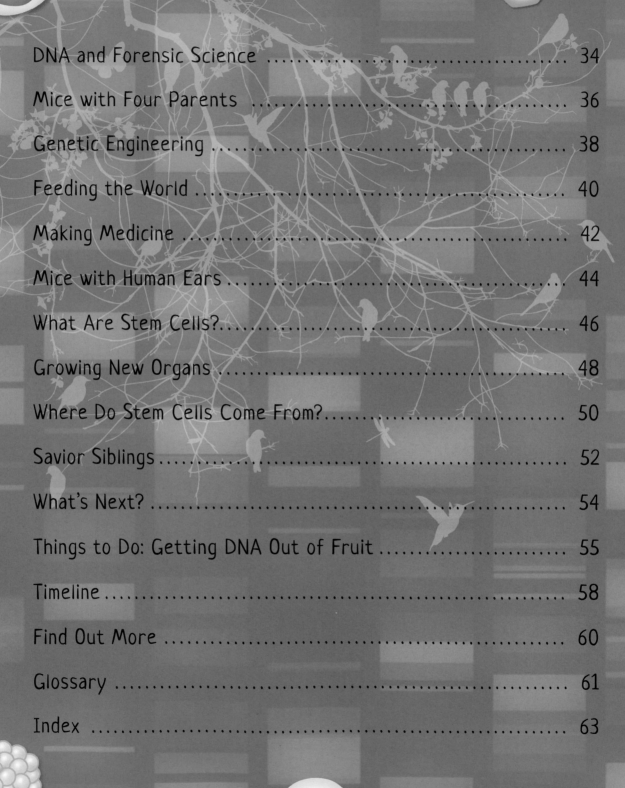

Introduction

DNA… **clones**…**stem cells**…**genetic engineering**… Each of these terms is in the news, but what do they mean? What's fact and what's fiction? What can we do now, and what might we be able to do in the future? Growing new body parts, using sheep to make medicines, cloning pets… It all sounds like science fiction. But these are facts, and they are amazing!

This book will take you from Charles Darwin and his Theory of Evolution, all the way to some of the most exciting developments in biology taking place now. This is a story about every one of your cells, and about everything that's ever been alive. This is the story of what makes you YOU. Come on into the book, and let me tell you a life story.

Let me tell you the story of life itself!

Charles Darwin and Evolution

Charles Darwin (1809–1882) studied all sorts of living things. He was interested in worms and pigeons, but he really loved beetles. When he was young, he was out looking for beetles one day. He spotted one he didn't have, so he picked it up. Then he found another new one, so he picked that up in the other hand. Then he found yet another new one, but he had run out of hands. So, what did he do? He put one in his mouth, of course, so he could pick up the third one!

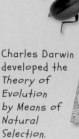

Charles Darwin developed the *Theory of Evolution by Means of Natural Selection.*

How evolution works:

Some types of animals and plants only have a few offspring, or babies. Others have many. Some have millions! So, why isn't the world filled up with rabbits or rats?

Darwin spent his whole life studying all kinds of living things. He made many discoveries, but his most famous one is called the *Theory of Evolution by Means of Natural Selection.* It explains how all the living things in the world today developed over a huge period of time from a few, much simpler living things.

ON

ORIGIN OF SPECIES

BY MEANS OF NATURAL SELECTION,

ON THE
PRESERVATION OF FAVOURED RACES IN THE STRUGGLE
FOR LIFE.

By CHARLES DARWIN, M.A.,

FELLOW OF THE ROYAL, GEOLOGICAL, LINNEAN, ETC., SOCIETIES;
AUTHOR OF 'JOURNAL OF RESEARCHES DURING H. M. S. BEAGLE'S VOYAGE
ROUND THE WORLD.'

LONDON:
ALBEMARLE STREET.

🐀 The answer is that almost all these babies die before they can **breed**. For most types of living things, this means their total **population** stays about the same all the time.

🐀 The babies, such as baby rats, are all different from each other. Some can run faster than others, have a better sense of smell, or have sharper teeth.

🐀 They all compete with each other for things such as, food, shelter, and mates, or breeding partners.

🐀 The most successful rats find the most food and the safest shelters, so they live long enough to breed. The rats that are slower or not as good at sniffing out food, die.

🐀 The rats that are able to breed pass on to their babies the characteristics that made them successful (being good at running, biting, or smelling).

🐀 Breeding goes on and on over many years. Over time, the rat population slowly changes into... super rats! They're so different from the original rats, they have become a new **species**.

Natural selection

This happened over and over again for millions of years—not just with rats, but with all living things. The world started off with just a few simple animals and plants. As time went on, more and more appeared. Now there are millions of different species.

One question Darwin couldn't answer, however, was why the rats were different from each other in the first place.

We know now that it's because of their DNA.

So, What Is This DNA Stuff, Anyway?

Your cells are too small to see without a microscope. In fact, 500 of them side by side would only measure 0.4 inches (1 cm). But each cell has about 6.5 feet (2 m) of DNA in it! Altogether, you have *thousands* of miles of DNA in your body.

> DNA is important. You need to know some details about DNA before so the rest of the book will be easier to understand.

What is DNA?

✳ Your body is made up of billions of cells.

✳ Every cell contains long threadlike things called **chromosomes**, which are made of a substance called **DNA**.

✳ Deoxyribonucleic acid, or DNA for short, is very long and thin. It's shaped like a twisted ladder—a shape sometimes called a **double helix**.

✳ The steps of the ladder are made of pairs of **molecules** called **bases**.

✳ There are four different bases, called **A**, **C**, **G**, and **T**. They fit together in pairs. A fits with T, and C fits with G.

✳ The order of the bases down one side of the ladder forms a code. It's a bit like an alphabet that has only four letters in it.

T (Thymine) ———

G (Guanine) ———

What does DNA do?

DNA is a set of instructions for making a living thing. Each instruction is called a **gene**. Each gene or combination of genes controls things about you, such as eye color, hair color, or nose shape. The order of the bases on the DNA makes up each gene. Each chromosome is made up by many genes. It seems incredible that something as simple as DNA can make a human, a tree, or a frog.

Although DNA was discovered in 1869, it took a long time before anyone realized how important it was. A four-letter alphabet seemed much too simple to control everything that happens inside a cell.

Surprisingly, only about ten percent of DNA actually makes up genes. The DNA that does not make genes, called "junk DNA," is still very important. Scientists now think that it helps to switch genes on and off at the right times. We also use junk DNA for **DNA fingerprinting**.

There's more about DNA later in the book.

A (Adenine)

C (Cytosine)

The Monk and the Pea Plants

At about the same time as Darwin was working on his ideas about evolution, Gregor Mendel was counting peas...

Mendel (1822–1884) was a monk who lived in a monastery in what is now the Czech Republic. He wanted to be a biology teacher as well as a monk. But he failed his exams twice, so he had to change his plans. He taught math and physics instead.

(Is that really easier?) He was in charge of the monastery gardens, and spent a lot of time experimenting on pea plants. He was interested in how things such as the color of the flowers or the length of the stems passed from one plant to its offspring.

Here's what Mendel did:

1. He took pollen from the flowers of a tall pea plant and put it into the flowers of a short pea plant.

2. He collected the seeds of the short pea plant and grew them to see if they turned into tall or short plants.

3. He found they were all tall.

4. He took pollen from one of these new tall plants and put it into the flowers of another new tall plant.

5. He collected the seeds of the new plant and grew them to see if they turned into tall or short plants.

6. This time, there were tall plants and short plants. There were about three times as many tall plants as short plants.

Mendel did this over and over. He always got the same results.

Gregor Mendel worked out the laws of inheritance before anyone knew genes existed.

A great discovery?

Mendel told other people about his work in 1865, but no one was very interested. It wasn't until 1900 that three separate scientists rediscovered the same thing and realized how important it was. Without knowing anything about DNA, Mendel had discovered genes.

Your Chromosomes and YOU

You are probably a little like each of your **biological parents**, but not exactly the same as them. Have you ever wondered why?

You began life when one cell from your mother, called an egg, and one cell from your father, called a sperm, joined together. Most cells in a human have 23 pairs of chromosomes. Sperm and eggs are special, because they each have 23 single chromosomes. This means that when they join, they make a cell with 23 pairs. So, you got half of each pair from your mom and the other half from your dad.

Now, you are obviously much bigger than just one cell. That single cell divided in two, then each of those divided over and over. You turned into a ball of cells called an **embryo**, and then into a baby. Now you are made of billions of cells.

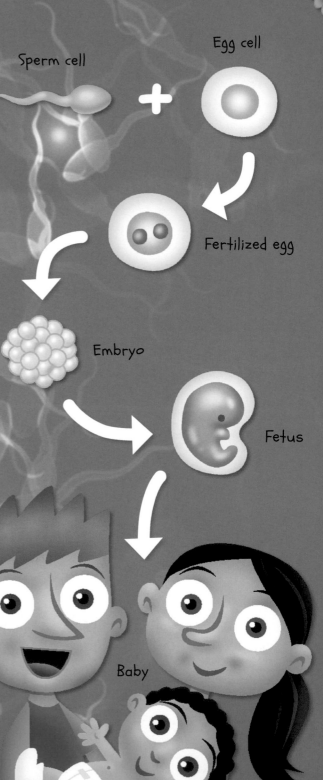

Sperm cell

Egg cell

Fertilized egg

Embryo

Fetus

Baby

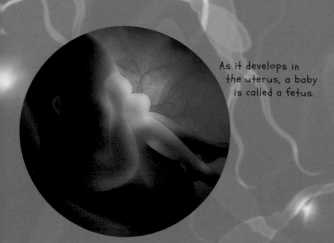

As it develops in the uterus, a baby is called a fetus.

But here's the REALLY amazing part!

How it works

Every time a cell is about to divide, it makes copies of all its chromosomes. This is so the new cells each get a complete set.

The two chromosomes that make up a pair contain genes that control the same things. So you get one copy of each gene from your dad and another copy from your mom. But the two copies might not be exactly the same. Different forms of the same gene are called alleles.

Let's look at the gene for eye color. To keep things simple, we'll only look at brown and blue eyes.

If both alleles make brown eyes, then you will have brown eyes.

If both alleles make blue eyes, then you will have blue eyes.

But what happens if one allele makes brown eyes, and the other one makes blue eyes? Do you end up with one blue eye and one brown eye? Are your eyes blue one day and brown the next? Of course not!

Usually one allele is stronger than the other, and that allele takes control. In this example, the allele for brown eyes is stronger than the allele for blue eyes.

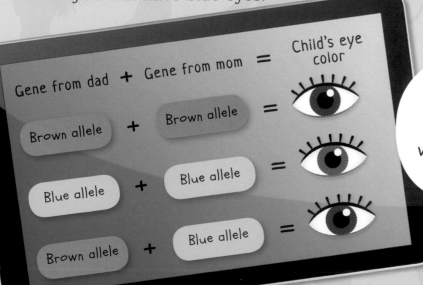

Gene from dad + Gene from mom = Child's eye color

Brown allele + Brown allele =

Blue allele + Blue allele =

Brown allele + Blue allele =

So, if you had one of each color allele, you would end up with brown eyes.

The Battle of the Sexes

You now know that you have 23 pairs of chromosomes in each cell. One is a pair of **sex chromosomes**. These come in two forms: X and Y. Boys have one X and one Y. Girls have two X chromosomes.

When sperm and eggs are made, they only get one of each pair of chromosomes.

Every egg gets an X. Sperm either get an X or a Y.

This means that the sex of a baby depends on which type of sperm joins with the egg. There are equal numbers of X sperm and Y sperm. This is why there are equal numbers of girls and boys born.

It's the same in almost all other mammals. In birds and butterflies though, males are XX and females are XY. Also, in some insects, females have two X chromosomes, males have one X, and there's no Y at all.

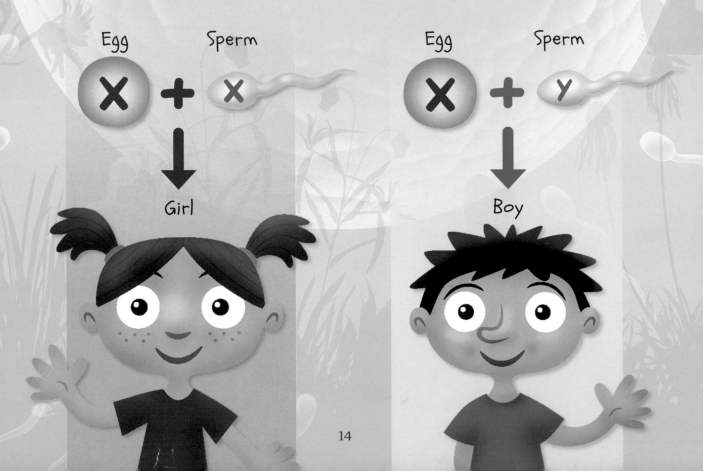

Egg Sperm
X + X
↓
Girl

Egg Sperm
X + Y
↓
Boy

Sometimes nature doesn't follow the recipe, and people end up with unusual numbers of sex chromosomes.

XYY is the combination that people have been most interested in. A study once suggested that prison populations had a higher percentage of men with XYY chromosomes than the non-prison population. Some lawyers even argued in court that their clients weren't responsible for their wrongdoing because the extra Y chromosome they had made them more likely to commit crimes. It wasn't a very good excuse. Most XYY men are law-abiding citizens, and current research suggests that the previous studies were incorrect.

Y have I got extra Xs?

Human embryos can't develop with just a Y chromosome. Although they can sometimes develop with just one X, or an X and two Ys (XYY), this can cause problems with development. Some women have three X chromosomes (XXX), but they don't seem to have many differences from women with two.

I don't know "Y" I keep stealing things...

This male chaffinch is XX.

Francis Crick

Maurice Wilkins

James Watson

The Great DNA Race

When they realized how important DNA was, scientist began research to determine exactly what it looked like and how it was put together. Different groups of scientists raced against each other to be the first to make this important discovery. They knew whoever won was going to be famous.

Francis Crick and James Watson worked at Cambridge University in the United Kingdom. They were supposed to be doing research in other areas, but they became very interested in DNA. They started to spend all their time on that. At King's College in London, England, Maurice Wilkins and Rosalind Franklin were also trying to find out more about DNA.

You couldn't have found four more different people! James Watson was a young American who had just come to Cambridge. He was very, very smart. In fact, back in the United States, he had started university when he was only 15 years old! Just 23 when he arrived at Cambridge, he was determined to find out what genes were.

Bet you never knew scientists had races!

English biologist Francis Crick was already working in Cambridge. He was also quite brilliant, but hadn't discovered anything important yet—and he had already reached the ripe old age of 35!

From bombs to DNA

Physicist Maurice Wilkins had been working for years in the same laboratory at King's College. During World War II, he had helped design the atomic bomb. In 1951, he had been looking at DNA for some time. It was his work that had made Watson and Crick interested in the subject.

Rosalind Franklin

British chemist Rosalind Franklin had been very happily living and working in Paris. When she came back to the United Kingdom to work, she found life very different. She and Maurice didn't like each other, so the lab at King's College wasn't a very happy workplace.

Women scientists in the 1950s

It was hard to be a female scientist in the 1950s. Some records suggest that Rosalind Franklin wasn't even allowed to have her lunch in the same room as the male scientists at King's College.

CANTEEN

MEN ONLY

17

Taking Photos of DNA

At Kings College, both Maurice Wilkins and Rosalind Franklin used x-rays to take special photos of DNA crystals. They don't look like regular photographs, so it's very hard to figure out exactly what they show. Wilkins was good at this, but Franklin was even better. She was a very serious scientist, and she always wanted a lot of evidence before she told other people about her results.

James Watson took a very different approach. He wanted to get results as fast as possible. Crick and Watson thought the best way to figure out what DNA looked like was to build models of it. They wanted to try to match their models to what other people had already discovered about DNA. Crick had already been using models like this in his other work.

The secret "borrowing" of Franklin's research

In March 1952, Watson went to see Wilkins to talk about DNA. While he was there, Wilkins showed him one of Franklin's best DNA photos without her permission. Watson learned a lot from looking at it.

On March 7, 1953, Watson and Crick finished a model that fit correctly with all the information known about DNA at the time, including from Franklin's photo.

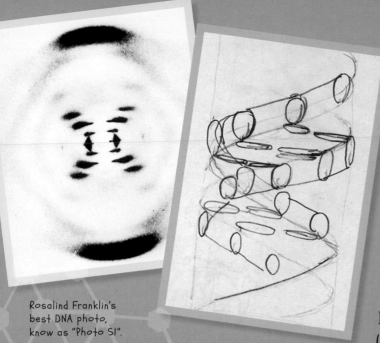

The structure that Watson and Crick figured out from the "borrowed" photograph.

Rosalind Franklin's best DNA photo, know as "Photo 51".

Winning the Nobel Prize

In 1962, Wilkins, Watson, and Crick were awarded a Nobel Prize for their work on DNA. Rosalind Franklin had died in 1958 of cancer (possibly because of all the work she did with x-rays). She was only 37 years old. The Nobel Prize is only given to living people, so she couldn't be given a share in it.

That day, Francis Crick went home and told his wife that he had found something very important. She didn't take him seriously though, because he was always saying things like that. But this time, he was right. Their model of the double helix shape of DNA was a great discovery, but it was another 25 years before experiments proved it to be correct. Sometimes, science is very slow!

The rest of this book is based on the amazing discovery made by these scientists.

The secret of life

When Watson and Crick realized they had won the race to find the structure of DNA, they went to the Eagle pub in Cambridge and announced that they had discovered "the secret of life."

DNA Double Helix 1953
"The secret of life"
For decades the Eagle was the local pub for scientists from the nearby Cavendish Laboratory.
It was here on February 28th 1953 that Francis Crick and James Watson first announced their discovery of how DNA carries genetic information.
Unveiled by James Watson
25th April 2003

The Human Genome Project

In 1990, scientists all over the world started work on a huge project called the **Human Genome Project**. They wanted to find out the order of all the bases in human DNA. This was a huge task. There were about 3 billion DNA bases to check! They expected the job to take 15 years, but they finished two years early in 2003 because advancements in computer technology had made the work go much faster.

Now that scientists know the correct order of the DNA bases, they know what each gene should look like. Scientists have discovered that

Part of a printout from an automatic DNA sequencing machine

irregular patterns in the DNA order can cause certain diseases. This is because a gene can't give the right instructions if it contains a mistake.

What does this mean?

The Human Genome Project means we can now test for the possibility of people developing certain genetic diseases before they get sick. Testing for an irregular gene could help a person prepare for, or even get treatment to prevent, an illness. However, some people do not wish to know if they will develop a devastating disease.

See pages 8-9 for an explanation of DNA bases.

Owning genes

There have also been some very strange results from the Human Genome Project.

Certain drug companies can "own" a gene if they are able to figure out the order of its DNA bases before anyone else. This means no one else can use that gene for research without the company's permission. The company can "own" a gene for 20 years after it's discovery!

That means, if a drug company found that you had a very useful gene and they figured out the order of the DNA bases on it first, the company could own that gene. They could make money from it, but you couldn't. The ethics of gene ownership is a hot topic of debate.

We're all the same, really!

One thing that the Human Genome Project has shown is just how alike all humans are. Over 99.9 percent of your DNA is exactly the same as every other person on the planet! More amazingly, you also share 98.5 percent of your DNA with chimps, and 97.5 percent with mice!

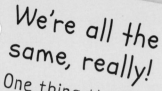

Even our mother can't tell us apart!

Embryo Selection

Some diseases caused by mistakes in DNA are passed on from parents to their children. If we know what mistake in the DNA to look for, it is possible to test parents to see if they have a chance of passing on these diseases. If there is a risk of passing on a genetic illness, the embryo can also be tested to see if it has the harmful gene. For couples who risk passing on a harmful gene, this information can be used to help them ensure their children will not develop this illness. This is called **embryo selection**.

Making babies

Couples at risk of passing on **inherited** diseases can choose to have children through a process called **in vitro fertilization**. This is a process in which eggs and sperm are mixed in a glass dish in a laboratory to create embryos. To ensure that genetic diseases are not passed on, they can choose to have the DNA of each embryo studied for irregularities.

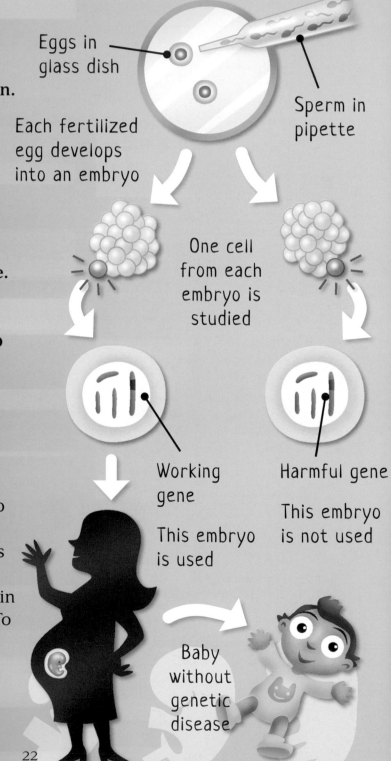

In vitro fertilization and embryo selection
(in vitro = in glass)

Eggs in glass dish

Sperm in pipette

Each fertilized egg develops into an embryo

One cell from each embryo is studied

Working gene

Harmful gene

This embryo is used

This embryo is not used

Baby without genetic disease

How it works

When a sperm and an egg join together, they make an embryo. The embryo starts to divide and multiply. One cell becomes two, two become four, four become eight, and so on.

Scientists can remove a single cell from each embryo without damaging it. They check its DNA for faults.

The embryo with no genetic faults is then transferred into the mother's **uterus**. It **implants** in the wall of the uterus, it can grow into a baby without the genetic disease.

As we become able to test for more and more faulty genes, we will be able to prevent more inherited diseases. Most people think this is a good thing.

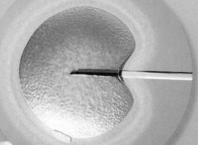

A single sperm can be injected into an egg.

But where do you stop once you start?

The right to choose

Selecting embryos to prevent diseases sounds like a good idea. But how far should we take gene selection? What about choosing whether you want to have a boy or a girl? Should you be able to say you don't want a baby who is color-blind? Or left-handed? Some people worry that we may have too much power to change what our children will be like in the future.

- ☑ Blue eyes
- ☒ Brown eyes
- ☒ Red hair
- ☑ Black hair
- ☑ Sporty
- ☑ Smart

Gene Therapy

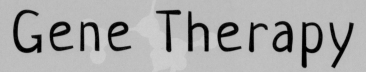

The Human Genome Project has allowed us to identify genes that cause some very serious illnesses. If scientists can repair or replace these genes, they might be able to cure some of these diseases. This is called **gene therapy**. This is a new field of treatment and is still being researched.

It has already cured some people.

How it works

1. Scientists have to make lots of copies of the gene in its normal, working form.

Normal gene

2. Next, they must smuggle the working gene into the person's cells that contain the harmful gene. Hopefully, the normal gene will take over from the faulty one.

Harmful gene

3. The normal gene is disguised as a faulty gene, hidden inside a virus altered to be harmless, or inside tiny bubbles of liquid fat.

Normal gene in fat bubble

Normal gene in harmless virus

4. The cells containing the harmful gene take in the viruses or fat bubbles.

Cell gets copies of normal gene

5. If everything goes as planned, the replacement gene goes to work in the cell, and the effect of the faulty gene disappears.

Scientists have tried to use this technique to treat, and even to cure, **cystic fibrosis**. They asked sufferers to breathe in the working genes, because cystic fibrosis affects the lungs. Unfortunately, this treatment has not been very successful so far. But research continues...

Remember, science can be slooooow!

Replacing genes

Since the 1990s, there have been many attempts at using gene therapy. It has been used to restore sight to people who suffer from a particular type of inherited blindness, and to treat some forms of cancer. It hasn't been the instant successs that scientists hoped for, but it's still a new field.

Genomic Medicine

This new field of medicine was made possible because of the Human Genome Project. It involves making personalized **drugs** for people, based on their genes.

Many people suffer from asthma, and use an inhaler to help them breathe.

One of the most common drugs used in an inhaler is called "albuterol" or "salbutamol." It helps treat people who suffer from asthma, a condition that makes it hard to breath. Inhalers containing this drug work by relaxing the muscles in the walls of the airway. This makes the airway tubes wider, so it's easier to breathe. Unfortunately, for some people, this particular medicine doesn't work. Looking at their genes can help explain why.

The muscles of some asthma sufferers contain a slightly different **protein** than normal. This difference came about because the gene that instructed the muscle to grow is also slightly different. These people can be given a different drug in their inhalers, which will do the same job. Doctors don't check a patient's DNA first to figure out which drug to use. They try the usual medicine first to see if it works.

What is a protein?

→ Your muscles, body tissue, bones, and organs are made of different proteins. Proteins are made of **amino acids**.

→ Your cells then use the amino acids to build all the different proteins they need.

A protein

A chain of amino acids

Amino acids are put together

→ Your body can make some of these proteins. To get others, you need to eat protein-rich foods such as meat, dairy products, nuts, seeds, and pulses (dried peas and beans).

→ Your DNA tells the cells which amino acids to put together, and in which order, to make the right protein.

Amino acids can fit together in different ways

All these foods contain protein

→ Your body breaks down the food during **digestion** to release the amino acids.

Amino acids are released

It's like using the same building blocks to build different models!

27

Clones

A **clone** is an exact copy idea of one person or other living thing. It is something you often read about in comics or see in science fiction films. Most clones in stories are scary or dangerous, but in real life clones aren't monsters at all. In fact, some of you reading this may be clones.

That surprised you, didn't it? But it's true. Honestly!

Fraternal or non-identical twins

Two eggs are released

They are fertilized by two sperm

They develop into two embryos

Each embryo develops into a non-identical baby

Identical twins

One egg is released

It is fertilized by one sperm

It develops into one embryo. The embryo splits in two

Each embryo develops into an identical baby

Conjoined twins

One egg is released

It is fertilized by one sperm

The embryo splits in two, but not completely

Each embryo develops into an identical baby, linked by some part of their bodies

Clones are living things that have identical DNA. All their genes are identical, which makes them… identical. This is how identical twins, or triplets, can be considered clones. Not all twins or triplets are clones, though. There are two types of twins: identical and non-identical, also called fraternal. Identical twins are always the same sex, and they look very similar. Non-identical twins can be the same sex or different sexes, and they don't always look alike.

How twins happen

Sometimes, two eggs are released from a woman's ovaries at the same time. If each of the eggs is fertilized by a sperm, each egg develops into an embryo, then a baby. The two babies are in the uterus at the same time, but they are no more alike than any other brothers or sisters. These are non-identical, or fraternal, twins.

Sometimes when a single egg has been fertilized normally by a single sperm, the embryo splits into two. This happens early in development when it is still just a tiny ball of cells. Each half develops into a complete, normal baby. Since they have the same DNA, they are identical twins.

Very occasionally the embryo does not split completely. This is how **conjoined twins** develop. The way they are linked depends on the part of the embryo that stays together. Conjoined twins used to be called "Siamese twins." The name came from the famous twins Chang and Eng Bunker who were born in 1811 in Siam, which is now called Thailand. They came to America as "curiosities" in a carnival and stayed to become farmers. They married sisters, and both men had families. The brothers died on the same day in 1874.

The famous Chang and Eng Bunker

Dolly the Sheep (1996–2003)

The most famous clone isn't a human; it's a sheep named Dolly. However, Dolly isn't a twin. She was cloned in a different way.

How Dolly was cloned

Finn Dorset ewe

Scottish Blackface ewe

Cell taken from udder

Unfertilized egg

Udder cell and "empty" egg are fused together by a tiny electric shock

Nucleus removed and destroyed

"Empty" egg with no DNA

Another tiny electric shock starts cell division, and an embryo develops

Embryo is implanted into the uterus of another Scottish Blackface ewe

Dolly is born.

She is a clone of the Finn Dorset ewe because all her DNA came from that sheep.

Making history

Dolly is famous because it was the first mammal to be cloned this way, although Professor John Gurdon cloned frogs in the 1960s and 1970s. Dolly was cloned near Edinburgh, Scotland in 1996, by a team of scientists led by Professor Ian Wilmut. He named the sheep after Dolly Parton, the famous country and western singer. Dolly the sheep gave birth to four lambs fathered by the same ram. They were just normal lambs, not clones.

Dolly got a lung disease that's normally found in much older sheep, and was put down in 2003 at age six. Sheep usually live to be 11 or 12, so Dolly died very young. Some scientists think it was because Dolly's DNA had come from a four-year-old sheep. That meant Dolly's DNA was already four years old when she was born, making her DNA actually 10 years old when she died.

How much do you love your pets?

Since Dolly was made, scientists have cloned cats, dogs, cows, and monkeys. Some very rich people have even had clones made of their pet cats and dogs when their pets died! Cloning dead pets isn't cheap. It costs about $150,000 per pet in the United States.

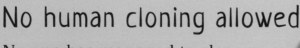

No human cloning allowed

No one has managed to clone a human yet. In fact, there are rules to stop this from happening in many countries and states around the world. This is because many people are concerned that cloning may not be used in an **ethical** way.

Stop! Catch that thief!

DNA Fingerprinting

Remember the "junk" DNA you learned about on page nine? It's time to find out just how useful it is. We can use it to find out who has committed a specific crime, who is related to who, and whether you are being charged too much for food in a restaurant.

The more closely related you are to someone, the more alike your junk DNA will be. To compare DNA, scientists take the junk DNA out of the cells in a blood sample. The DNA is chopped up and placed in some special jelly. Electricity is passed through the jelly, which makes the parts of DNA move apart. This makes a pattern of stripes. The more alike the patterns of two people's junk DNA, the more closely related they are.

This technique is often used to help solve crimes. For example, a sample of DNA can be taken from a bloodstain. The DNA in the stain can be compared with DNA samples from suspects to look for a matching pattern.

Solving crimes

DNA fingerprinting was first used to solve a murder in 1988. It proved that a teenage boy who had been charged with a double murder must be innocent because his DNA didn't match the samples from the bodies. It also proved that another man must be the murderer because his DNA matched the sample. That man was sent to jail for 30 years.

DNA pattern

Cold cases

DNA fingerprinting can even be used on bloodstains that are years old. Some crimes from long ago have recently been solved using new DNA evidence. DNA has also been used to prove that some people who were jailed in the past for various crimes were actually innocent. More than 160 people have been freed because DNA fingerprinting showed they hadn't carried out the crimes for which they were in prison.

I'm free!

C'est bon!

BUDGET CAVIAR

$$$

Caviar is a dish made of the raw eggs from a fish called a sturgeon.

Caviar

But what about that restaurant bill?

Some expensive restaurants sell a luxury food called caviar. Traditionally, caviar is a dish made of the raw eggs from a particular fish—the sturgeon. However, DNA fingerprinting of the fish eggs shows some restaurants mix sturgeon eggs with much cheaper fish eggs. They save on costs and make more money by still charging a lot.

Sturgeon

DNA and Forensic Science

Many people love reading crime novels, or watching crime shows on TV. But do these shows resemble reality at all? What can the police and **forensic scientists** really figure out using only DNA? And is DNA evidence always reliable?

DNA fingerprinting has been used as evidence in hundreds of cases since 1986. It has helped solve murders, serious violent crimes, break-ins, and burglaries. On TV, the forensic scientists get results in a couple of hours. In real life, it can actually take weeks!

So, yes, DNA really is used to solve crimes.

Combined DNA Index System (CODIS)

The FBI in the United States keeps a combined database of DNA samples collected from convicted criminals, people who have been arrested, and crime scene evidence. As of October 2015, CODIS has more than 14.8 million DNA records, which have assisted in more than 285,450 investigations.

Dusting for fingerprints

Finding DNA evidence

Fingerprints

Hair

Fibers from clothing

Blood

Hopefully, you've got an **alibi**...

Where do we find DNA?

DNA can now be picked up from a single hair or a few skin cells. It is copied in a machine until there's enough for DNA fingerprinting. This is great because even the tiniest trace of evidence is useful, but it also means that the people collecting the samples have to be very careful they don't **contaminate** the crime scene.

Contamination really is a serious problem. If you gave someone a hug, then they robbed someone's house while still wearing the clothes you hugged them in, your DNA would be all over the crime scene!

Mice with Four Parents

How can that make sense?

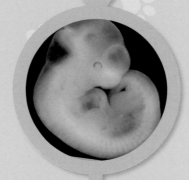

Sometimes two embryos join together at a very early stage of development to make one baby. In a way, it's the opposite of how you get identical twins.

Scientists can mix embryos together in the laboratory to create animals that have four parents. They can join two mouse embryos: one from parents with black hair, and one from parents with white hair. This makes a mouse with a mixture of black hair and white hair. This is useful, because it tells the scientists which parts of each embryo turn into which parts of the adult.

Interestingly, the new mouse also has two kinds of DNA. It gets one kind from each original embryo. When a living thing has two kinds of DNA, it is called a **chimera**. Amazingly, it occasionally happens naturally in humans.

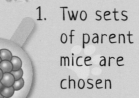

1. Two sets of parent mice are chosen

2. Two mouse embryos are joined together

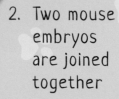

3. A mouse fetus forms

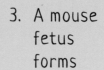

4. A mouse with both white hair and black hair is born

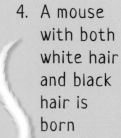

Human chimeras

Sometimes in humans, the embryos of twins join together in the early stages of development and end up as one person. The person probably wouldn't ever know that it had happened. You wouldn't be able to tell anything was different about that person just by looking at them. The secret would be in their DNA.

The story of Lydia Fairchild

Lydia Fairchild lived in the United States. She had two children and was pregnant with a third, when her marriage broke up. She was asked to take a DNA test to help prove that her husband was the children's father.

Wow!

The results showed that he was the father, but she wasn't the mother!

How could this be? Police thought maybe she had stolen the children, and they took them away from her. When her third baby was born, its DNA was tested right away. Again, the results said she wasn't this baby's mother either. Everyone realized that this was impossible, since doctors had seen her give birth. No one could explain what had happened.

When they did more tests, they found that DNA from some parts of her body matched her children's DNA, but DNA from other parts didn't. She had two different groups of DNA. They discovered she was a chimera—fraternal, or non-identical, twins who had ended up as a single person.

1. Two eggs are released

2. They are fertilized by two sperm

3. They develop into two embryos

4. The two embryos fuse together to make a single embryo

5. The embryo develops into one baby, but with two sets of DNA: one full set from each original embryo

I'm a catfish! Get it?

Genetic Engineering

The subject of **genetic engineering** is often in the news, but what does it really mean? Genetic engineering means taking a gene from one type of plant or animal, and putting it into another plant or animal.

It sounds as if this could create some very strange animals and plants. But in real life, genetic engineering doesn't result in new animals—no half-cat, half-fish, or carrots and apples growing from the same plant.

That's not really what happens!

Genetic changes

The first food to be changed by genetic engineering was a type of tomato. It was given an extra gene to slow down the rotting process. Most tomatoes are picked when they are still green so they don't rot before they are sold. The changed tomato could be picked when it was ripe, yet stay fresh for a long time in stores.

However, the company that invented these genetically engineered tomatoes stopped growing them after just a few years. This was because they hadn't chosen a very good type of tomato to work with. Even though their tomatoes stayed fresh for longer, they didn't taste as good as other types of non-genetically engineered tomatoes.

From science lab to supermarket

In supermarkets today, it has been estimated that 75 percent of processed foods contain at least some genetically modified ingredients. These include various types of cooking oil, crackers, and chocolate. Milk, eggs, and meat sometimes come from animals fed genetically modified feed. This makes identifying all genetically modified ingredients on food labels difficult. Labeling these ingredients is not currently required in the United States and Canada.

Genetically
engineered crops

ANiMAL
FEED

Hungry cows eat the
genetically modified feed

The cows
are milked

The milk is made
into cheese

EASY CHEESE

INGREDIENTS:
Milk, Salt, Stabilizers
and Preservatives

Feeding the World

One of the reasons scientists are so interested in making genetically engineered plants is because the world's population is growing. Genetic engineering can help grow enough food to feed more and more people.

Plants such as rice and wheat can be genetically modified to become **resistant** to insects and other pests; to survive **droughts** or floods; or to contain extra vitamins. This means fewer crops will fail, and more people can be fed using the same amount of land.

Some people believe that genetically engineering crops is the only way to make sure there will be enough food for everyone in the future.

How many?

10

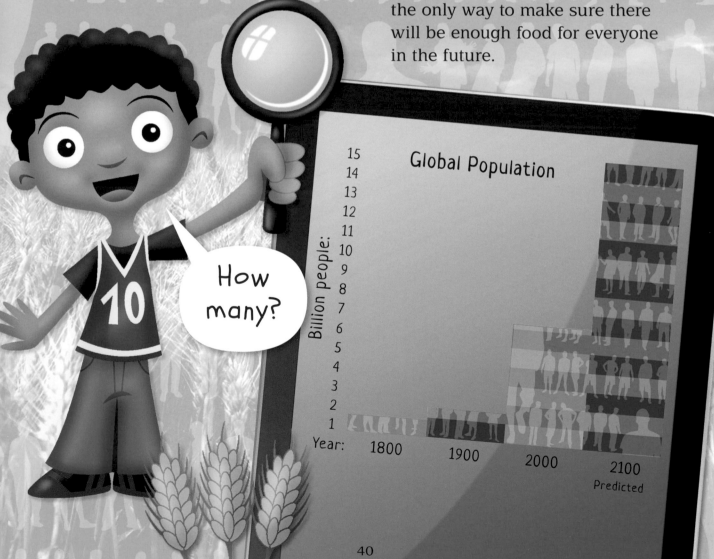

Global Population

Billion people:
15
14
13
12
11
10
9
8
7
6
5
4
3
2
1

Year: 1800   1900   2000   2100
Predicted

Super weeds and other problems

Other people are worried that if we start growing lots of genetically modified crops, we may accidentally cause much bigger problems in the future.

Adding genes to plants could have unexpected **side effects** on the animals or people that eat them. The modified plants could breed with weeds, creating "super weeds" that would be very hard to kill. Then, according to Darwin's Theory of Evolution, any insects or pests that manage to survive on plants that are supposed to kill them will eventually become "super pests."

Countries around the world are cautiously moving ahead with genetically engineered crops, while scientists figure out all the possible risks and benefits.

Are you calling me a weed?

Modifying mosquitoes

Scientists are using genetic modification to reduce the number of mosquitoes that carry dengue fever, a severe disease. They have genetically engineered male mosquitoes to produce offspring that will die before they grow into adults that will carry the disease. If this proves to be safe and effective, they hope the same method can be used on the four species of mosquito that spread malaria, a disease that kills half a million people every year.

Making Medicine

Advances in genetic engineering have allowed scientists to use **bacteria** to make chemicals the human body needs to work properly. For example, we can now make **insulin**, which is used to treat the disease **diabetes**.

People who suffer from **type 1 diabetes** cannot produce the chemical insulin on their own. In the past, insulin was taken from the **pancreas** of a **slaughtered** pig, cow, or sheep. Today, genetic engineering allows us to grow bacteria that produces human insulin.

To do this, the human gene that creates insulin is put into a special kind of bacteria, which is then grown in huge tanks. The bacteria produce insulin, which scientists can then **purify** for use in humans. A lot of other chemicals can be made this way, including a **human growth hormone**, which is used to help children who aren't growing properly.

I wonder how tall it could make me?

How insulin is made

The gene for insulin is cut out of human DNA.

The gene is inserted into a bacterium.

The bacterium is put in a tank where it grows into many bacteria. All of them contain the human gene for insulin.

The insulin is extracted and purified. It is then ready for humans to use.

Another amazing sheep

Just as bacteria can be modified, animals can be, too. In 1990, scientists genetically engineered a sheep called Tracy. They added a human gene to Tracy's sheep genes. This gave Tracy the ability to make a special protein in her milk normally only produced by humans. This protein could be taken out of her milk and used by doctors to treat the disease cystic fibrosis.

Six years later the same scientists produced Dolly the sheep. Dolly's creators were also trying to learn how to safely clone a sheep with an extra human gene, like Tracy.

Scientists have also created glowing mice, rats, cats, pigs, and even monkeys. They hope that studying these animals will help them understand more about how moving genes between species might help fight human diseases.

Proteins are the building blocks that make bones, tissues, and organs.

Glow-in-the-dark pets!

Today, you can even buy genetically engineered pets! For example, GloFish are goldfish that have been genetically modified to glow in the dark. A gene that makes sea jellies glow in different colors was added.

It's very hard to get to sleep with the lights on!

43

Mice with Human Ears

Pardon?

If you look up "Vacanti mouse" on the Internet, there's a famous picture of a very strange-looking mouse. It doesn't have human ears on its head. It just has normal mouse ears. However, it does have what looks like a human ear on its back. Except it isn't actually a human ear at all. Confused? Let me explain...

The thing on the mouse's back is the shape of a human ear, but it isn't made of human cells. It isn't made of mouse cells, either. It's made of cow **cartilage** cells. Cartilage is the bendable stuff in your ears and at the end of your nose. Scientists put an ear-shaped mold under the mouse's skin, then injected cow cartilage cells into the mold. The cells grew over the mold to create the final ear shape. It doesn't work as an actual ear though. The mouse can't hear anything with it.

But, why did they do it?

Well, human ears often get damaged because they stick out to catch sound waves. They're also very hard to repair because they're such a complicated shape. Surgeons often say it would be great to have spare ears to transplant onto people who have lost or damaged their own. So, scientists began to experiment to see if this might be possible.

Could we grow spare ears on humans?

We could, but it wouldn't work with cow cells. This is because your **immune system** would attack the new ears as if they were a dangerous infection. They would probably turn black and fall off! Your immune system is what fights off germs. It recognizes and destroys cells that shouldn't be in you. It helps keep you from getting sick, but it also means it will try to destroy organs transplanted from another person.

However, scientists can now produce new ears using human cartilage cells. The new ears are grown on a special ear "**scaffold**" in a dish, not on a mouse. Scientists are beginning to transplant these ears onto children born with abnormal or missing ears.

Because they make the new ear using the children's own cells, the ears shouldn't be rejected by the children's immune systems. The same technique is also being used to grow new noses and replacement **arteries**.

A replacement ear being grown

What Are Stem Cells?

You might hear the words **stem cells** being mentioned in the news. There is a lot of interest in what scientists might be able to do with them. So, what are they?

Stem cells are cells in a living thing which haven't decided yet what kind of job they're going to do. They still have time to turn into any type of cell. They can also divide many times.

How are cells different?

All living things start out as just a single cell. Most living things end up as billions of cells, all working together. To get from a single cell to the final fully-grown human, cat, potato, or rose bush, the following things need to happen:

1. The cells need to multiply. First, the single cell divides into two cells.

2. Then, the two cells grow until they are full-sized. They divide again, resulting in four cells, then eight, and so on.

3. This happens over and over again.

4. The cells must become different from each other.

5. If cells did not become different, you wouldn't have different body parts such as skin, muscles, and bone. You'd just be a blob!

6. Most living things, including you, are made of a lot of different types of cells. Each cell does a different job.

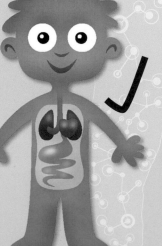

Genetic information

All of your cells have a full set of genes in them, but most cells only use a few of those genes. For instance, white blood cells only use the genes that make them good at fighting diseases. They don't use the same genes as skin cells, even though both types of cells have identical genes.

Once a cell has "decided" what it's going to be, the genes it won't use are switched off. They can't usually be switched on again. Usually this also means the cells won't divide very much any more.

Unlike cells that perform particular jobs, stem cells can still turn into anything and keep dividing. Scientists are excited because stem cells can be used to make body parts.

Stem cells are the raw materials for building the body.

A single fertilized egg has the genes to make the whole organism.

Growing New Organs

Scientists want to use stem cells to figure out how to control the genes that make cells do certain jobs. If they can learn how to do this, it might mean they could grow new organs, such as kidneys and hearts, for transplant into people. Right now, people with failing organs must wait on a list until a human organ donor becomes available.

Organ transplants

Every day in North America, more than 20 people die while waiting on a list for an organ transplant. Those fortunate enough to receive a donor organ must take drugs for the rest of their lives to keep their immune systems from attacking the donor organ. If new organs could be grown from a patient's own cells, there would be no need to wait for human donors and no need to take drugs for a lifetime.

Heart

Kidneys

Intestines

Will there be one if I need it?

Saving lives

In 2008, an organ was actually grown for the first time. Scientists grew a windpipe, which is the tube that takes air to your lungs, using a patient's own cells. Doctors replaced a damaged windpipe in a woman who was very ill.

In that case, they took a donor windpipe and used chemicals to get rid of all the windpipe cells. This left only the cartilage behind. They then used stem cells taken from the sick patient to grow new windpipe cells over the cartilage. The operation was a success. The patient was cured and did not need to take any drugs.

Healing hearts

Doctors have also injected stem cells into damaged hearts to help repair them after heart attacks. Research is still being carried out, but doctors hope that one day they will be able to cure **heart failure** this way.

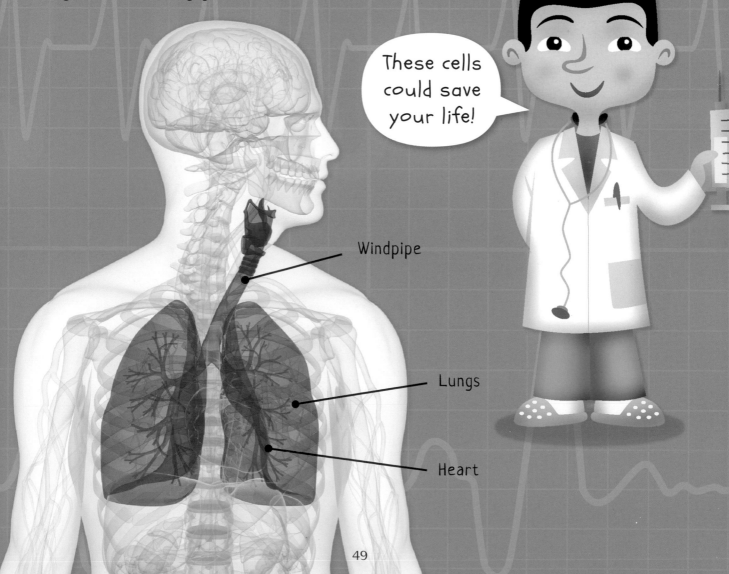

These cells could save your life!

Windpipe

Lungs

Heart

Where Do Stem Cells Come From?

Stem cell research seems to offer a lot of promising solutions to human health problems that include organ disease, spinal cord injuries, diseases of the brain and central nervous system, and birth defects. There are three sources for extracting stem cells.

Stem cells can come from:

1. Embryos. When a sperm and an egg join they make a new single cell. An embryo is the tiny ball of stem cells made when the new cell starts to divide and multiply.

2. Blood from a baby's **umbilical cord**.

3. Some types of adult cells. One example is bone marrow, which is the fatty stuff inside your bones that makes your blood.

Embryo stem cells

An embryo is a ball of cells at the earliest growth stage in the development of a human. Early research depended on using stem cells from embryos because they had not yet been "switched on" to do particular jobs. Their use was **controversial** because the embryo had to be destroyed. It posed a moral question for many people who felt destroying an embryo was destroying a human life.

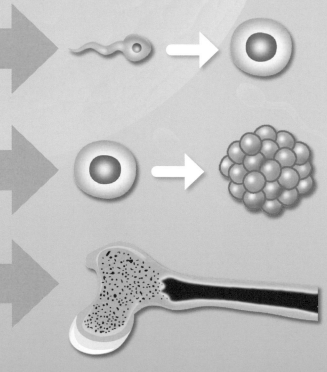

Umbilical cord stem cells

The umbilical cord is what joins a baby to its mother when it's in her uterus. The baby gets food and oxygen through it until it's born. Once the baby is born, it doesn't need the cord any more, and it's cut off. Your belly button is the scar where your umbilical cord was attached to your mother.

The cord usually just gets thrown away, but it has a lot of blood cells and stem cells in it. This is the easiest way of collecting stem cells.

Adult stem cells

Before 2007, using cells from adults was difficult. This is because some of the adult genes have already been switched off. Fortunately, a way was discovered to switch them on again. This allows the cells to be turned into other types of cells. Doctors hope to be able to take cells from your skin and grow them into new bone, or a heart, or a liver.

You have to come out sometime you know!

Umbilical cord

The baby doesn't need its umbilical cord anymore.

51

Savior Siblings

Fanconi anemia is a rare and very serious disease. It is sometimes passed on from parents to their children. Until recently, there was no effective treatment for most sufferers, and many died when they were children.

The Nash family's daughter Molly was born with the disease. In 2000, when Molly was six, doctors in Chicago helped her parents to **conceive** the world's first savior sibling. Sperm and eggs from her parents were mixed in a laboratory and developed into tiny embryos. The embryos were tested to find one that did not have the disease, and also had the right cells to help cure Molly. This embryo was put into Molly's mother's uterus. It grew into a perfectly healthy baby. His name is Adam Nash.

Baby to the rescue

When Adam was born, his umbilical cord was cut. Instead of throwing it away, stem cells were collected from it. The cells were used to replace Molly's bone marrow, which wasn't working properly. Adam's stem cells cured Molly.

How did it work?

1. An embryo that is a suitable DNA match is chosen. It grows into baby Adam.

2. When he is born, Adam's umbilical cord is cut off.

3. Stem cells are collected from the blood in the cord.

4. The cells are grown in a laboratory until there are a lot more stem cells.

5. Adam's stem cells are used to replace Molly's bone marrow.

Molly is cured!

This treatment was, and still is, controversial. People have strong opinions for and against the practice.

⚛ Some news articles about this kind of treatment are not written accurately. They make it seem like the "savior" baby is physically hurt in some way in order to treat its sibling. This is not true.

⚛ Some people worry that a "savior" child will not feel as wanted or loved as their sibling, since they were conceived because their stem cells were needed.

⚛ To increase the chances of getting an embryo that is a good DNA match, scientists make many embryos to choose from. The unused embryos are sometimes discarded. Some people see this as destroying human life.

Everyone is allowed to have their own opinion about how they feel about this kind of treatment. If it were you, how would you feel if you knew you were conceived to try to save your big brother's or sister's life?

What's Next?

You are living at a very exciting time for biology and medicine

In your lifetime, doctors may be able to use what scientists are learning about DNA to cure many diseases. We may be able to use stem cells to grow new organs or repair damaged spinal cords to help people walk again.

Of course, when dealing with human life, there are always moral and ethical questions to consider about what we should or should not do. What are the consequences of cloning people? Should people be allowed to choose their future baby's hair, eye, or skin color? Is it a good idea for the DNA of all sorts of plants and animals to be mixed together?

The future is bright

We can't do all of these things yet, but it's important to talk about these things before they are possible. Perhaps we can agree on rules about what scientists should and should not do. It's also important that people—like you, who might make the rules one day—understand what it's all about. Hopefully, this book has made you want to find out more.

Just think—some of you might turn out to be the scientists who make another big discovery about DNA and genetics. After all, now that you know what makes you YOU...

what's stopping you?

Things to Do: Getting DNA Out of Fruit

Warning: This experiment involves hot water and a chemical called denatured alcohol, a fuel that is poisonous and should only be used under adult supervision.

What you need:

- **Fruit:**
  About 2 oz. (50 g) hulled strawberries
  or half a peeled kiwi fruit
  or half a peeled banana

- **Extraction fluid:**
  Mix about a half a cup (100 ml) of water, with 2 tsp. (10 ml) of dishwashing liquid and half a teaspoon (3 g) of salt.

- **Coffee filter paper**

- **Strainer**

- **Two large empty bowls**

- **One bowl of water at about 140° F (60° C) (Need adult supervision):**
  (Two parts boiling water to one part cold water is close enough.)

- **Resealable plastic bag**

- **Ice**

- **Fresh pineapple juice:**
  About half a teaspoon (3 ml)

- **A clean, tall and narrow glass**

- **Important: Only use with adult supervision.**
  Ice-cold denatured alcohol:
  Denatured alcohol can only be bought from a hardware store by an adult. This should be put in the freezer in a plastic bottle. A glass bottle could explode!

Fruit

Extraction fluid

Coffee filter paper

Strainer

Plastic bag

Bowl of hot water

Two large bowls

Pineapple juice

Ice

Tall glass

Denatured alcohol

55

What to do:

1. Put the fruit (either strawberries, kiwi, or banana) into the plastic bag and seal it.

Squash the fruit

2. Squash the fruit inside the bag until it is mushy.

3. Add 1/4 cup (50 ml) of the extraction fluid you made to the bag. Seal it again, and give it a squish to mix it in with the fruit.

Add the extraction fuid

4. Put the sealed bag in a bowl of hot water (about 140° F (60° C) for 15 minutes.

Heat the fruit and fluid

5. While you are waiting, put some ice and cold water into one of the empty bowls.

Get the icy water ready

6. After 15 minutes, take the plastic bag out of the bowl of hot water, Put it in the bowl of icy water to cool down.

Cool the fruit and fluid

7. Put the coffee filter in the strainer. Put the strainer over the remaining clean, empty bowl.

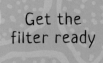

Get the filter ready

8. When cool, pour the contents of the sealed bag through the coffee filter.

Filter the fruit mixture

9. Remove the coffee filter and pour the liquid from the bowl into a tall, narrow glass. You only need about 2 tsp (10 ml).

Pour the liquid into the glass

10. Add the pineapple juice and mix. Leave for two minutes.

Add pineapple juice

11. With an adult's help, get the denatured alcohol from the freezer. Pour it very slowly onto the fruit liquid in the glass.

Very slowly add chilled denatured alcohol

12. It will form a purple layer on top of the fruit layer.

You might be surprised how much DNA you get!

Whitish strands of DNA should appear, rising from the fruit layer into the alcohol.

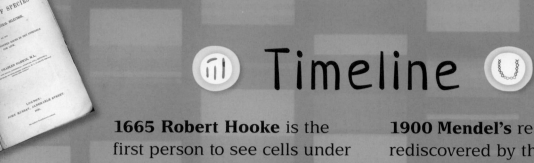

Timeline

1665 Robert Hooke is the first person to see cells under a microscope.

1831 Robert Browne discovers the cell nucleus (the "brain" of the cell).

1843 Karl Wilhelm von Nägeli discovers the "ideoplasma"—what we now know as chromosomes.

1856 Gregor Mendel publishes the results of his pea experiments. No one pays attention or realizes the importance of what he has discovered.

1857 Charles Darwin publishes *On the Origin of Species by Means of Natural Selection.*

1869 Friedrich Miescher isolates something he calls "nuclein": from white blood cells in pus. This will later be renamed DNA.

1900 Mendel's results are rediscovered by three other scientists, who realize how important they are.

1952 Robert Briggs and **Thomas King** clone a leopard frog by taking the nucleus from an embryo cell and putting it into an egg cell from which they have removed the nucleus.

1953 James Watson and **Francis Crick** publish a paper in the science journal *Nature*, describing the structure of DNA. Rosalind Franklin and Maurice Wilkins also publish a paper in *Nature*, describing their own results on DNA.

1958 Rosalind Franklin dies of cancer, possibly caused by the high doses of x-rays she used in her work.

1958 John Gurdon clones a frog by transferring a nucleus from an adult frog cell to an egg cell from which he had removed the nucleus. This shows that all the genes must still be present in adult cells.

1962 James Watson, Francis Crick and **Maurice Wilkins** are awarded the Nobel Prize for their work on DNA. Rosalind Franklin is not, because it is only ever given to living people.

1984 Alec Jeffreys develops DNA fingerprinting.

1990 Ashanti DeSilva becomes the first person to be treated by gene therapy.

1996 Dolly the sheep is born, cloned by Professor Ian Wilmut at the Roslin Institute in Scotland.

2000 Adam Nash, the world's first "savior sibling" is born.

2003 Dolly the sheep dies.

2008 Claudia Castillo receives a new windpipe, grown from her own stem cells.

2012 The first use of stem cells from embryos takes place, in a trial to treat a form of sight loss called Stargardt's Disease.

2012 The first genomic medicine to treat Cystic Fibrosis is approved.

2012 John Gurdon and **Shinya Yamanaka** are awarded the Nobel Prize for research which led to stem cell therapy and the cloning of Dolly the sheep.

Find Out More

Read

Traits and Attributes by Natalie Hyde (Crabtree Publishing, 2010)

DNA by Natalie Hyde (Crabtree Publishing, 2010)

Genetic Engineering by Marina Cohen, (Crabtree Publishing, 2010)

Watch

Cracking the Code of Life (PBS, 2001)

Follow cutting-edge scientists as they discover the exact letter-by-letter sequence that makes up the human genome.

This video gives a brief history of the foundation of life. Find out more about DNA at:
http://www.popsci.com/science/article/2013-03/watch-absolutely-beautiful-animated-explainer-dna

Join characters Tim and Moby as they introduce the world of DNA to you. Watch the video, then have fun taking a quiz or testing your knowledge in different activities.
www.brainpop.com/health/freemovies/dna/

Learn more about genetics with these educational videos, games, and activities at:
www.neok12.com/Genetics.htm

Visit

The DNA discovery center at the Field Museum in Chicago, Illinois. See scientists conducting DNA research before your eyes!
www.fieldmuseum.org/at-the-field/exhibitions/dna-discovery-center

The DNA Learning Center in Cold Spring Harbor, New York to explore exhibits and conduct laboratory experiments.
www.dnalc.org

Log on to:

This is a great interactive site that allows you to do all sorts of DNA related things in a virtual lab. Try your hand at DNA fingerprinting, or clone a mouse!
http://learn.genetics.utah.edu

Explore these interactive online exhibits to learn all about how DNA and genetics work.
http://genetics.thetech.org/online-exhibits

Try your hand at making a copy of a chromosome with the DNA game!
www.nobelprize.org/educational/medicine/dna_double_helix

Glossary

alibi Reason why you could not have possibly committed a crime

amino acids Chemical building blocks used by your body to make **proteins**

arteries Muscular tubes that lead blood away from the heart and to the body

bacteria Microorganisms (living things) made of just one cell

bases The chemicals in DNA that make up the four-letter alphabet of the genetic code. The letters are A, C, G and T.

biological parents The two people who gave you your DNA

breed Reproduce

cartilage Tough, flexible tissue that makes up your nose, throat, and ears

chimera Single animal or person produced when two embryos merge at a very early stage of development

chromosomes Long strands of DNA found in the nucleus of cells

clones Two or more living things with exactly the same DNA, such as identical twins

conceive To become pregnant

conjoined twins Identical twins that are physically joined at some part of the body

contaminate Spread DNA or other substances in a place where they shouldn't be

controversial Creates strong public opinion for and against it

cystic fibrosis Serious lung disease caused by a fault in a person's DNA

diabetes Disease caused when a person's body cannot control insulin levels

digestion Breaking down food in the body into a form that can be used or removed

double helix A coiled structure of double-stranded DNA molecules

DNA Deoxyribonucleic acid: the chemical that makes up genes and chromosomes

DNA fingerprinting Way of comparing DNA from different people to find out if they are related. Can also be used to compare DNA from crime scenes with DNA from suspects.

donor Somebody who gives away a body part, an organ, tissue, or blood for the treatment of other people

droughts Long periods to time when there is little or no rain

drugs Substance used to treat, prevent, or diagnose a disease and to lessen pain

embryo Tiny ball of cells that develops into a new organism

embryo selection Checking the chromosomes of an embryo to find one that is free from a genetic disease

ethical Morally acceptable.

evolution Process by which all living things on the planet developed over huge lengths of time from a few, much simpler species

ewe An adult female sheep

Fanconi anemia Disease that causes many kinds of cancer

forensic scientist Someone who studies the evidence left at a crime scene

gene Length of DNA that controls characteristics such as the color of your eyes

gene therapy The process of replacing a missing or faulty gene to treat or cure a disease

genetic engineering Process of inserting a gene from one species into a completely different species

heart failure Result of damage to the heart, meaning it stops working completely

Human Genome Project International project to figure out the entire genetic code of a human being

human growth hormone Chemical that tells our bodies when and how much to grow

immune system Body's system for fighting disease, which can also cause rejection of transplanted organs

implant Embed or place something in the body

inherited Received as a result of genes being passed from parent to offspring

insulin Hormone, or chemical, that controls the body's blood sugar, or glucose, levels

in vitro fertilization Mixing eggs and sperm in the laboratory to produce embryos

molecule Smallest physical unit of a substance

moral Considered right and wrong

nucleus The "brain" of a cell, where all the genetic material is stored

pancreas Organ that creates hormones, or chemicals, including insulin

population All of the organisms that live in a particular area

proteins Building blocks that make body tissue, bones, and organs

purify Remove anything harmful or unwanted

resistant Unharmed by the damaging effects of something

savior sibling Brother or sister chosen because they are genetically compatible with an ill older sibling, and may be able to help them by donating stem cells

scaffold Temporary supporting framework

sex chromosomes Pair of chromosomes (XX or XY) which determine the sex of a baby

side effects Unexpected and usually undesirable results of an experiment or treatment

slaughter Kill an animal

species Group of animals or plants that share lots of characteristics and can breed to produce fertile offspring

stem cells Cells that haven't yet decided what to be when they grow up. They can turn into any type of cell in the organism.

type 1 diabetes Disease in which the body is no longer able to process blood sugar, or glucose

umbilical cord Cord through which a baby in the uterus gets its food and oxygen from its mother. Usually thrown away after birth, but contains lots of stem cells.

uterus Womb